CHARACTER MATTERS

R. E. Myers

Good Year Books

An Imprint of Addison-Wesley Educational Publishers, Inc.

Dedication

In loving memory of my parents, who did their best to make me a better citizen.

Good Year Books

are available for most basic curriculum subjects plus many enrichment areas. For more Good Year Books, contact your local bookseller or educational dealer. For a complete catalog with information about other Good Year Books, please write:

Good Year Books
1900 East Lake Avenue
Glenview, IL 60025

Cover photos by Eric Futran.
Book design and cover art by Karen Kohn and Associates, Ltd.
Copyright © 1999 Good Year Books, an imprint of Addison-Wesley Educational Publishers, Inc.
All Rights Reserved.
Printed in the United States of America.

0-673-58644-8

1 2 3 4 5 6 7 8 9 - ML - 05 04 03 02 01 00 99

Preface

Character Matters was written because I feel that there must be more dialogue in the schools, especially in grades 6–8, about how to develop a more civil society. There is ample evidence that our young people need to show more respect for people and institutions. We must engage them in discussions about the responsibilities of citizens in our society, preferably before they reach high school.

The approach here is not to preach about the virtues of kindness, civic responsibility, honesty, civility, and so on. On the contrary, as a result of encountering the units in this book, your students are to discover and rediscover for themselves some of the precepts that they have been exposed to at home, at school, and in religious settings. This can be accomplished by means of discussion and investigation. By thinking about the stories and ideas presented in the units, young people can gain some important insights about what their lives can and should be in the twenty-first century.

The concepts presented in *Character Matters* are probably the most important ones in our culture. "Love" is not treated directly, but it is implied in the majority of the positive concepts. There are a few negative concepts, such as prejudice, but they are in the distinct minority. What is important, in my view, is for young people to be shown positive models of civil behavior. The stories in this book point up some of the ordinary ways people demonstrate their goodwill and their ethical character. We know that for as long as people have communicated in language that stories have carried a message more powerfully than any other vehicle.

So, while avoiding a didactive approach, this book endeavors to direct the attention of your students to the ideas in our society that have defined it at its highest level. Yes, we badly need ideals—and also the right kinds of idols. We teachers have to be concerned with encouraging our students to be better citizens because they are striving to be better people.

The units of this book are not designed to be used simply as discrete lessons; they should be starting points for discussion, and then deeper discussion, about the fundamental ideas of a civil society. The units can lead to additional learning associated with history, literature, art, mathematics, and even science. Use your judgment about when to administer a unit. No sequencing is implied in the order in which the units appear in any section of the book.

One of the distinguishing features of this book is its variety. Your students are invited to engage in many kinds of activities after reading the stories and/or responding to the games, puzzles, and quizzes that are presented to them. There is a chance that one or more of these activities may appeal to each of the differing personalities in your class.

The stories in this book are meant to have a high degree of believability. If they don't seem to, change them and make them more acceptable to your students.

I hope that your students can find something in the stories that rings true with respect to the forces and events in their lives. If any of the stories are not relevant to the lives of the young people in your classroom, please skip them. By examining an unpromising unit, however, you may get an idea of how to spark a meaningful discussion about that topic. I sincerely hope that you will modify any of the units to make them fit your students' abilities and backgrounds better. Above all, the units in this book are meant to open the eyes and minds of young people about civil behavior.

Contents

Working with Others — 62

Attitudes — 86

CHARACTER MATTERS
Personal Growth

This first section about personal growth offers a variety of concepts for your students to consider, from honesty with oneself to independence. The emphasis is on moral growth. The approach is to personally involve each student with a moral issue. For example, in the activity "Personality," most students will not give honest answers to all six questions. In the second part of the unit, they are asked to reflect on their answers a week later and to record differences in their answers. The experience should be instructional to those students who have already begun to deceive themselves. (Of course, we all do, to some extent.)

If such units as "Cheating the Cheater" and "Selfish Giving" are too sophisticated for your class, they can be presented later, after your students have worked on "Honest to Goodness," "Fake," and "Reversal" and have thereby learned more about their own behavior.

Honest to Goodness

Ohmigosh!" exclaimed Mr. Abtin. He turned around and went back into the post office. The clerk was finishing a transaction with a customer, and Mr. Abtin waited until she was done.

"I think a mistake was made when I was here a minute ago," Mr. Abtin began. The clerk's expression changed slightly, but she waited for Mr. Abtin to explain.

"If I'm not mistaken, you gave me change for five dollars, but I'm sure that I only gave you a dollar bill for that thirty-two-cent stamp. I remember having only a dollar on me when I came in."

"Oh, thank you very much. You must be right," the clerk said, with an embarrassed smile.

Mr. Abtin's behavior wasn't unusual. When most people realize that something doesn't belong to them, they will return the money or property.

When the teacher asks who threw the spitwad and no one answers, is the guilty party being dishonest or just cowardly—or maybe just protecting himself or herself? Explain your answer.

If you see a person in line ahead of you at the supermarket drop a five-dollar bill, is it dishonest to pick up the money and put it in your pocket?

When you write a report, is it dishonest to copy what the encyclopedia said about a subject without putting quotation marks around the words you have copied?

Does honesty mean giving a full day's work when you are hired to work eight hours cleaning up a house to be rented? Aren't you entitled to goof off a little?

CHARACTER

It's Your Life

Occasionally, we do or say something that isn't quite right, but we figure it's what lots of people do or that it won't make much difference to anyone if we behave that way. Sometimes it happens in a game, when we cheat a little; and it can also happen when the temptation is too strong to resist, like when we look over the shoulder of someone who has the answer on a test. Often we resist the temptation because if we are caught, the price will be too high.

Are the following actions dishonest? Explain why you think they are or are not.

Saying you took one piece of candy when you really took more.

Having someone at home do most (or all) of a homework assignment for you.

Fibbing about your age to get into a movie.

Saying you've done something you haven't done.

Taking money from your parent's wallet, and telling yourself you'll put the money back later.

Telling your parents it was someone else's idea when your gang got into trouble, even though you were all for it.

Not returning money when a clerk gives you back too much change.

Let's consider some of these situations in more depth. Have you ever said that you took just one piece of candy or only one cookie when you really took two or three? If so, what prompted you to say that you took only one?

Are you more likely to fib when you think no one can really know if you are telling the truth? Are you more likely to stretch the truth when you think people would disapprove of your behavior if they knew what you did?

Is it very wrong to take money from your mother's purse? Why?

If you need a little money, what are some ways of getting it?

What you say or do affects other people as well as yourself. Would you say that the greatest harm in being dishonest is that it injures your self-pride? Or would you say that the harm comes from deceiving others? Take a position, and write down the main points of your argument. Then find someone with an opposing view, and debate the matter.

CHARACTER

Personality

Each of us has an idea of the kind of person he or she is, and this sense of ourselves increases as we interact with people. Occasionally, we'll be one way in one situation and quite a different way in another situation. Most of the time, however, we are fairly consistent.

To see what kind of person you are, give forthright answers to these questions.

Do you enjoy being the center of attention, or would you rather just be someone in the group?

Would you rather make new friends, or would you prefer to be always with people you know very well?

Are you more comfortable telling someone how to do something or receiving instructions yourself?

Is it easier for you to make up an excuse or to apologize when you've made a mistake?

Which do you enjoy more—finding someone else's mistake, or discovering a mistake you have made and correcting it?

If you had your choice, would you rather flip a coin to see who will be the winner or compete with someone to determine who wins?

Put this sheet of paper some place where you won't lose it. In one week, reread the questions and your answers. Do you still want to respond to the questions in the same way? Write "yes" or "no" after the questions below. If you have changed your mind, explain why.

Do you enjoy being the center of attention, or would you rather just be someone in the group?

Would you rather make new friends, or would you prefer to be always with people you know very well?

Are you more comfortable telling someone how to do something or receiving instructions yourself?

Is it easier for you to make up an excuse or to apologize when you've made a mistake?

Which do you enjoy more—finding someone else's mistake, or discovering a mistake you have made and correcting it?

If you had your choice, would you rather flip a coin to see who will be the winner or compete with someone to determine who wins?

The exercise you have just completed is about only you, but it indicates how you interact with other people. How you have responded to it is a matter of how honest you are with yourself—how well you know yourself. If you didn't change any of your responses, either you know yourself well or you are kidding yourself. You might ask someone who knows you well if you have been honest with yourself.

CHARACTER

Cheating the Cheater

Let's pretend that most people cheat, even if only once in a great while. Let's go even further and pretend that once you cheated, although you may have forgotten all about it. It's not honorable, but people do cheat—claiming the rules of the game are different from what they really are, squeezing in ahead of other people in line, peeking at the answer to a quiz in the back of a magazine, standing on their toes when their height is being measured, and on and on. That kind of cheating usually doesn't have dire consequences.

What kinds of cheating are more serious?

Would you ever cheat:

at Solitaire?   Why?

in Checkers?   Why?

on a test?   Why?

on a book report?   Why?

in a race?   Why?

What is the best way to cheat:

a genius?

a crook?

a gossip?

a cheater?

a pompous fool?

a fortune teller?

a charlatan?

What happens to people who are cheated, generally speaking?

What happens to people who cheat?

Follow-Up to "Cheating the Cheater"

In order to make the questions about cheating more personal, you might have your students do some role-playing. For example, for the question about cheating on a test, the cheater could be trying to involve a classmate who doesn't want to cooperate. In role playing an instance of cheating in a race, there can be an official or a spectator and two or three competitors. Ask your students which of the five situations could be dramatized. (Solitaire could be ruled out, since it calls for only one actor.) Or you can ask for suggestions about incidents your students have witnessed or participated in.

Accusations of cheating start very early in a child's life and seem to persist through old age. The topic is worth pursuing in every area of ethical behavior. It is often prominent in political news, so this unit can be tied to discussions of current events.

Fake!

Gordon had a problem. Ever since he told his classmates that the zircon he found was a diamond, they regarded anything he told them with suspicion. Gordon became known as "Gordon the Fake." It didn't help that Nathan remembered when Gordon first arrived at school and told everyone he'd had a horse where he used to live. Nathan bumped into someone who knew Gordon in the other town. Not only did Gordon not have a horse; he was terribly embarrassed one day at his former school when the other students found out he was afraid of horses. Gordon's family couldn't afford to keep a horse anyway. They were too poor.

What advice would you give Gordon?

How can you tell if the following things are fake or genuine:

A diamond?

Ice cream?

A gold necklace?

A slice of bacon?

Perfume?

A painting by a famous artist?

Vanilla extract?

A smile?

A threat?

A promise?

A rumor about a friend?

A peace offer?

A love note?

The autograph of a star?

On the back of this piece of paper, write two or three paragraphs about why it is important to be a genuine person.

Shame

Shame is an unpleasant word. We don't like to hear it. The idea of shame bothers us. People used to say, "Shame on you!" Nobody wanted to be told that. Do you hear that expression any more?

What is the difference between shame and embarrassment? Is it a matter of degree, or are they two different feelings?

What word is the opposite of shame?

Name three things you do so that you won't be ashamed of yourself.

Is there something you would do if you weren't concerned about feeling ashamed if people found out you did it?

Which is more shameful?

Being ignorant or being overweight? Why?

Being cruel or being a liar? Why?

Being a bully or being a cheater? Why?

Being poor or being weak? Why?

Being a thief or being lazy? Why?

People have been ashamed of poverty, obesity, stupidity, and ugliness. They are sometimes even ashamed of being wrong. What role does fear of shame play in your life? Is it bad to be ashamed?

Excuses

When something goes wrong, we look for a reason. Often the thing that goes wrong can't be avoided, but frequently it is our own fault. When we are embarrassed by something we did, we may come up with an excuse, an alibi. It is natural to look for an excuse when the fault is principally ours, but some people are more prone to offer excuses than are others.

What is a good excuse for spilling milk at the table?

Why is it a good excuse?

What is a good excuse for not going to school?

Why is it a good excuse?

What is a good excuse for knocking over a lamp?

Why is it a good excuse?

What is a good excuse for oversleeping?

Why is it a good excuse?

What is a good excuse for kicking someone?

Why is it a good excuse?

What is a good excuse for forgetting someone's birthday?

Why is it a good excuse?

What is a good excuse for missing a shot in basketball?

Why is it a good excuse?

What is a good excuse for running in the hallway?

Why is it a good excuse?

What is a good excuse for losing your temper?

Why is it a good excuse?

What is a poor excuse for the following behaviors? Explain why each is not a good excuse.

Not stopping at a stop sign while riding a bike

Using bad language

Not responding to a friend's letter

Cutting in front of people in line

Failing to turn in an assignment

Quitting a game when you are losing

Getting the names of people you know confused

Are there times when you need to have an excuse? Describe them.

Are there times when an excuse makes everything worse? When?

Follow-Up to "Excuses"

Eight sentences have been broken into three parts each and scrambled in three columns. Have your students unscramble them. The original sentences can be pieced together fairly easily because some groups of words have capital letters, some will be relative clauses, and some will be predicates. These are the original sentences, each pertaining to some aspect of excuse-making.

When putting the sentences together, your students probably won't come up with the exact eight sentences. If they do get some right, fine. If not, they can at least have fun trying to come up with sentences that make sense or are amusing.

Shuffled Syntax Answers

Some people who make mistakes get red in the face.

All of us, if innocent, hate to be accused.

Some parents blame the teachers because the kids are dumb.

Big brothers make good scapegoats for little brats.

Politicians are very good at passing the buck.

Some teachers blame the parents when everything goes wrong.

Traffic cops, to their amusement, hear some crazy stories.

Persons with good alibis could still be guilty.

CHARACTER

Shuffled Syntax

The following groups of words were originally eight separate sentences, but they have been jumbled into three columns. See if you can put the sentences together again. Write the correct sentences at the bottom of this page.

Some people	with good alibis	Some parents
when everything goes wrong	All of us,	get red in the face
Persons	for little brats	Traffic cops,
to their amusement,	Some teachers	who make mistakes
because the kids are dumb	Politicians	if innocent,
make good scapegoats	could still be guilty	Big brothers
blame the teachers	are very good	at passing the buck
hate to be accused	hear some crazy stories	blame the parents

CHARACTER

Extending

*I*n the same way that an amoeba must extend itself to get food and to survive, people must extend themselves to grow physically, intellectually, socially, and spiritually.

What are the consequences if you don't extend yourself physically?

What are the consequences if you don't extend yourself intellectually?

What are the consequences if you don't extend yourself socially?

What are the consequences if you don't extend yourself spiritually?

A famous basketball player once said, "Each year I try to expand my learning experience by taking on a new challenge. I don't want to become a stagnant person." What challenge can you take on? On the back of this piece of paper, describe what you will do and how you will do it. In some detail, tell how taking on this challenge will change your life. Quite often, changing one part of your life will change almost all of the other parts as well.

Reversal

C oach Brown had told himself not to think about it, but here he was, walking back to the locker room with his players at halftime, and it crept back into his mind. Many of his players, especially those who had been in the game, were thinking of it too.

It was only two years ago. His school, Westview High, was only two years old, and it was playing in the AAA football league for the first time. There was only about a minute left to play, and Corn Valley High was ahead, 52–0. Because they were playing against Corn Valley's second- and third-team players, and because they were trying hard, Westview's team had managed to reach the opponent's three-yard line. With a touchdown imminent, Corn Valley's Coach Warren sent in his first-team defense, who throttled the Westview attempt. Corn Valley won, 52–0. Coach Brown, the Westview team, and a number of spectators were upset by Coach Warren's poor sportsmanship.

Many of Westview's players and supporters were thinking of revenge at the start of this year's game. Westview now had the best running back in the league and four linemen who would probably be named to the all-league team. The first half had borne out the hopes of the Westview partisans. Westview scored the first three times they had the ball, and then they

Copyright © Addison-Wesley Educational Publishers, Inc.

recovered a fumble for another score and intercepted a pass for a fifth touchdown before the half. Corn Valley hadn't been able to move the ball at all, and the score was 35–0.

Coach Brown was thinking about the game two years before, and then he began thinking about trying to keep his team healthy for the playoffs. Sure, they probably could rack up more points than CV had two years ago, but Coach Brown knew something about the feelings of the coaches and players of a team that is outclassed in every way. A big score would mean those on the CV side would be humiliated.

In the dressing room, Coach Brown quietly told his team that the reserves would have a chance to get some experience in the second half. Although his star back could improve his statistics with more yardage and touchdowns by playing more, Coach Brown didn't even have to say anything to him. He could tell by the boy's expression that, if given the choice, he would prefer to see a teammate get some playing time and would not enjoy rubbing CV's nose in the dirt.

What do you think Coach Warren said to Coach Brown after the game?

Is revenge usually sweet? Explain.

Sometimes, no matter how many substitutes a coach puts into the game, his team continues to roll up the score and trounce the opponent. In such cases, it appears that the coach didn't have any mercy for the opposing team, but that may not have been true. What is it that coaches and players on the losing side most want to avoid? If you need to, use another piece of paper to write your answer.

Smile

We can find out what is inside a house by entering it. We can find out what is inside a can that doesn't have a label by opening it. But can we tell what is inside a smile? Literally, smiles may involve teeth, mouths, cheeks, and eyes, but they signify something else, something inside the person.

Can you depict what is inside a smile in a symbolic or realistic way? Think about what a smile represents, and then sketch what is inside of a smile.

What were you trying to show in your sketch?

Now think of the smile of a prominent person. It can be the smile of a mayor, business owner, religious leader, governor, principal, television star, or anyone else who is well known. Draw a symbolic or realistic sketch of what is inside that person's smile.

Sketch the smile of someone you know very well.

Whose smile do you like most of all the people you know? Why?

Did you choose that person's smile for the one you just drew? Why or why not?

What you have done in sketching a person's smile, in either a realistic or a symbolic way, is express what you feel about that person's sincerity. A smile can disguise true feelings, or it can reveal honest feelings and attitudes. For example, if you had a hunch that a certain person's smile is false, you could have drawn a face with a smile and then behind it, in a lighter shade or a different color, you could have drawn a frown.

On the back of this piece of paper, make a sketch of your own smile.

Who is in Control?

You may have more or less control over your decisions than you think. Perhaps you think that you alone make almost all of your decisions. But you could be wrong about how crucial your wishes, opinions, and feelings are. How much say do you really have in:

choosing what you wear?

determining where you will live?

electing a school officer?

purchasing a car?

selecting someone to marry?

choosing an occupation?

What are the critical elements in making decisions about everyday living? Name at least four.

Did you include the element of chance? If not, why not?

What are the critical elements in making decisions about your community?

What are the critical elements in determining how the country is run?

Selfish Giving

Have you ever received a present or a favor from someone and felt that the person was getting more satisfaction from the giving than you were from the receiving? While some individuals derive a great deal of satisfaction out of making others happy with gifts, a few also get a feeling of superiority from being the giver.

Some people enjoy giving presents and are genuinely generous, but they don't like to receive gifts. Do you know anyone like that? Why do you suppose that person doesn't enjoy receiving gifts?

Which of these acts are examples of "selfish giving"? Explain why they are or are not good examples of that behavior.

Giving your seat to an elderly person

Giving away the cream-filled chocolates in your box of candy if you don't like cream-filled chocolates

Giving an electric guitar to your grandmother

Bringing home a quart of your favorite ice cream for dessert

Buying two tickets for a concert, and giving one to a classmate you'd like to be friends with

Giving half of your lunch to a friend who has lost his or hers

Giving so you'll be thanked and the person will be grateful to you

Are there any animals that are selfish givers? Name them. Then draw a picture of the animal giving selfishly.

A New World

The world is changing fast. Some of the changes are helping people. Other changes don't seem to be helping people. There are changes in the way we eat and play and in the way we talk and travel. Sometimes people like the changes. Sometimes they don't like the changes at all.

Let's imagine the world is going to have some more changes.

What might happen if children could watch television only on Saturday?

What might happen if people kept getting bigger and bigger?

What might happen if no one could wear the color red?

What might happen if all the birds died?

What might happen if everyone always told the truth?

Follow-Up to "A New World"

"The Consequences of Truth"

The final question of the unit is, "What might happen if everyone always told the truth?" There are many implications and possibilities inherent in an absolutely truthful world, some salutary and some disastrous.

Your students can explore two or three of those possibilities by role-playing situations in which people interact in altogether truthful ways. Perhaps the best procedure is to have students discuss their ideas of the consequences of a completely truthful society. Advise them to stay away from ideas that come from movies or television shows. The ideas that have the most promise can be dramatized by the students suggesting them (with cohorts of their choice assisting them) or by others willing to do the role-playing.

If the ideas don't emerge naturally, don't attempt the activity.

CHARACTER MATTERS
Concern for Others

Courtesy, civility, respect for the rights of others, and consideration of others are behaviors that help describe the kind of citizen we are striving to produce. They are what visitors notice first, and they therefore cause outsiders to regard a society as "refined" or not. Even though such virtues as honesty, truthfulness, and forgiveness may be more important, surface impressions influence the outside world in the many ways it deals with a society.

It is especially important to preview the stories in this section. They include one about the nearly hysterical substitute ("Nettie Speaks Up") and one about a bully ("Once Too Often"). The story about the family who lost everything in a fire ("A Great Big Heart") is, fortunately, so typical of the generous and compassionate spirit of people that you probably have had a similar incident in your community.

Her First Day

It was Kim's first day in class, and she felt a little frightened. She, along with her parents and five brothers and sisters, had just arrived in America a week ago. After their ship had docked, they cleared customs, and two hours later they were in a huge airplane flying to Minneapolis, a city in the Midwest. They were now living in a suburb of Minneapolis. Many of the people Kim had known in her village had been brought here by a local church. But even though she was grateful to be in America, Kim couldn't speak English and she felt very strange.

Knowing Kim couldn't speak a word of English, Mrs. Knowles, the teacher, had assigned her a seat near the front of the room, where she could quickly assist Kim. Across the aisle from Kim was Margaret, one of the best students in the class. Mrs. Knowles noticed that Margaret was watching Kim and smiling at her. At first, being shy, Kim didn't look at Margaret or return the smile.

At lunchtime, Mrs. Knowles asked Margaret to show Kim where the restroom was and how to use the cafeteria. Margaret and Kim sat together throughout lunch. With gestures and facial expressions, they were able to communicate.

After lunch, Mrs. Knowles gave Margaret permission to slide her desk next to Kim's and to help Kim whenever it was necessary. At the end of the day, Margaret promised to bring some pictures of her family to class so that Kim could learn more about Margaret and her family. Kim went home feeling less fearful of her new school.

What quality did Margaret exhibit in her behavior toward Kim? Do young people usually behave like Margaret did when newcomers arrive in class? How do you and your classmates act toward people who are different from you?

How old do you think Kim was?

Was she of average height, short, or tall?

What do you think Margaret looked like?

How was she dressed?

Draw a picture of the two girls. They can be at their desks, in the cafeteria, or on the playground. Put as much detail as you can into your picture.

Once Too Often

Although Tom had warned him any number of times, Leon kept tormenting Prentice during recess. Prentice would be minding his own business, and, suddenly, he'd feel a glob of mud hit his back. Or he'd be in the outfield chasing a fly ball, and from the sidelines Leon would call him a bungler, a butterfingered jerk, or worse. Tom warned Leon to be careful because Prentice studied martial arts and was a skillful fighter, even though he looked puny.

Prentice had always been picked on because he was shorter and lighter than the other boys in his classes. Realizing his son was getting pushed around, Prentice's father had suggested a martial arts class, and Prentice surprised everyone by being one of the best students in the class.

The martial arts teacher repeatedly told the students to use their moves and throws only in self-defense, so Prentice had never used his skills outside of the class. One rainy morning, as Prentice and Tom were heading for the bus, Leon came up behind Prentice and shoved him hard. Prentice fell into a mud puddle. Several children laughed.

"Lay off, Leon!" shouted Prentice, as he got up dripping water and mud.

"What ya goin' to do about it, Prentice?" challenged Leon. He extended his arm to shove Prentice again.

All of a sudden, Leon was sprawled face-down in the mud, and Prentice was looking down at him.

"I warned you," Tom said.

A lack of respect was shown in two ways in this story. What were they?

Have you ever observed a sequence of events similar to the one in this story? Describe it.

It is said that a bully is covering up his or her own feelings of inferiority by picking on people he or she believes won't stand up to him or her. Not all bullies try to physically intimidate and hurt their victims. What are two or three other ways bullies pick on people?

How could the muddy confrontation have been avoided?

Thinking of Others

Here are seven statements that you should consider carefully. They have to do with a few of the ways people interact with each other. If you don't have a ready answer, discuss the statements and their implications with other students. Write your reactions below each statement.

People are likely to expect more politeness on overseas flights on airplanes than on subways in large cities.

Check-out clerks in supermarkets show more respect to handicapped persons than do drivers who deliver pizzas.

Barbers are more courteous to musicians than are train conductors.

People who go to Italian restaurants are more likely to be rude to waiters than are people who go to Mexican restaurants.

Authors of mystery novels are likely to be more sensitive to the needs of the elderly than are most people.

Individuals older than thirty-five are generally more courteous than are younger persons.

It's always a good idea to ask permission before you take the last piece of candy.

Follow-Up to "Thinking of Others"

In most conversations and group discussions, we tend to "put our two cents in" before the speaker has finished talking. "The Automatic Chairperson" will help develop the skills of listening courteously and intelligently to others. It enforces a kind of discipline upon the listeners that facilitates courtesy and productive discussion.

"Double Talk" can also be used as a follow-up for "Thinking of Others." It is the kind of activity that needs to be carefully administered because of the number of students who will be talking.

The Automatic Chairperson

About eight to ten students are in a circle to discuss a topic of vital interest. You can be a member of the group or an observer. Begin by placing the "chairperson," an easily grasped object, such as a wooden carving about ten inches long, in front of one person. The presence of the "chairperson" entitles that person to speak about the topic without being interrupted. When the speaker is finished, he or she passes the "chairperson" to the next person in the circle. Anyone can decline to speak by saying, "I pass."

After the "chairperson" has made at least one round trip, it may be passed directly to any student who wishes to contribute to the discussion. This technique emphasizes courteous listening because everyone is assured of having a chance to speak, so students can concentrate on what others say.

Double Talk

You might also have your students engage in the related exercise, "Double Talk." Have them pair off and face each other. Then tell them to relate, simultaneously, their experiences of the past twenty-four hours. They should talk without pausing for three minutes. After you have stopped them, have your students take turns recalling what their partners said.

This exercise dramatically shows the results of thinking about what you want to say while someone else is speaking.

A Great Big Heart

It was in mid-January, the coldest morning of the new year. The Cogdills were shivering on the sidewalk. Five hours earlier, before dawn, their modest home at the edge of the city had burned to the ground. The firefighters saved all five members of the Cogdill family—but nothing else. There was nothing but a couple of walls and some rubble where a five-room cottage had been.

Mr. Cogdill worked as a day laborer on a construction project, and Mrs. Cogdill worked in a laundromat. Their children, ages two, four, and five, went to a day-care center five days a week. The family had no savings and no homeowner's insurance.

Even before the story of the Cogdills' tragedy was reported on the radio and television news, neighbors and others in the community had collected food and clothing for the destitute family. One neighbor offered to take them into her house until other housing arrangements could be made. After the news story, people from all over the state began sending money to the Cogdills.

Americans are quick to help others in times of emergency. In recent years, floods, earthquakes, fires, and hurricanes have devastated areas of the country, and the response—both public and private—has been immediate and generous.

There is a federal relief agency that provides food, shelter, clothing, and medical supplies, as well as money, to the victims of disasters. What is its name?

The Red Cross and other organizations offer relief to victims of floods, hurricanes, wars, volcanic eruptions, famines, hurricanes, and other disasters throughout the world. Without these organizations, countless people would die or suffer needlessly. Where do the people who work for these organizations come from?

Some of the people who work for relief organizations are paid, but many more volunteer their services. Would you work for an organization like the Red Cross? Why or why not?

Follow-Up to "A Great Big Heart"

You might offer the magic square puzzle to your students after their discussion of compassion. The subject of this magic square, "love," is presented in its universal and impersonal sense.

If most of your students successfully solve the puzzle, have them create their own magic squares. As an extra challenge, they could try to connect the four words (**"love," "over," "veto,"** and **"Eros"**) in some way.

Magic Square

A magic square is composed of words whose letters spell the same word down as they do from left to right. Read the definitions of the four words below, and fill in the words in the boxes of the square. If they read the same down as they do across, you've solved the puzzle.

Very strong positive feeling; deep affection or devotion

The opposite of *under*

To prevent, prohibit, or forbid

The Greek god whose mother was Aphrodite

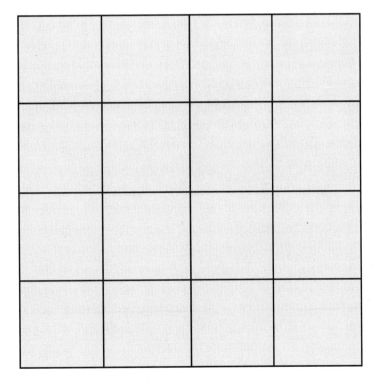

Gentle on Your Mind

There is an old country-and-western song entitled "Gentle on My Mind." If you haven't heard the song, you may be wondering what the title means. Does it mean that something rests gently on the mind of the songwriter? Or could it mean that his mind is dwelling on something that is gentle? Ordinarily, we speak of food, school, clothing, mischief, boys, girls, and the like being on our minds. We usually don't talk about having lazy, happy, sloppy, cute, mellow, sour, or noise on our minds.

What could it mean to have "happy" on your mind? What kind of tempo would you give a song with that title?

What could it mean to have "soft" on your mind? What kinds of tempo and harmony would you give a song of that title?

What could it mean to have "dry" on your mind? What music would go well with a song of that title?

The idea of "gentle on my mind" communicates something pleasant. *Gentle* is the kind of word that agrees with our ideas of what thoughtful, peace-loving people should be. We don't usually think of a lion as being gentle, but within their pride (group) adult lions are typically gentle and loving. When it comes to people, who do we usually think of as being gentle? Place a check (✔) next to the people you think of as being gentle.

Golfers	Police	Chefs
Librarians	Nurses	Farmers
Dentists	Ballroom dancers	Protesters
Stamp collectors	Joggers	Musicians
Accountants	Ventriloquists	Television repair people
Bankers	Army generals	Doctors
Reporters	Airplane pilots	Actors

What kinds of people do you think of as being particularly gentle?

What kinds of people do you think should be gentler than they usually are?

A Helping Hand

Several spokes on a wheel of Ted's bicycle were bent and one was broken after he skidded on the gravel path and rammed his bike into a big oak tree. Paul, the boy next door, noticed the damage and asked Ted if he knew how to fix the wheel.

"I haven't done it before," Ted said a little sheepishly.

"No trick at all if you have the tool. I have one, Ted. I'll go get it," Paul offered.

In less than an hour, Ted's bicycle was fixed. He smiled happily at Paul, grateful that Paul didn't make him feel more like a klutz than he did already.

A few weeks later, Paul mentioned to Ted that he'd like to be able to throw a curve ball. Ted, who could pitch quite well, volunteered to teach Paul how. Ted spent an hour during each of the next four days teaching Paul the technique of throwing a curve ball. Paul could throw a curve by the time of the tryouts for the team, but he probably never would be the pitcher that Ted was. Paul excelled in mechanical things, and Ted was an athlete.

Some people are too shy or feel too embarrassed to ask for help.
Often they are missing an opportunity both to learn something and
to find out that most people are eager to help friends, acquaintances, and even
strangers. Do you know anyone who hates to ask for help? Why do you think
that is?

One of the reasons some people don't like to ask for help is that it makes them
feel inferior. What is a good way of helping someone without making that
person feel inferior?

Gory Movie

A film company that specialized in gory thrillers received approval to shoot a film at the high school. Some of the townspeople felt that the content of the film and the language used in it were not suitable for a town like theirs. They wrote letters protesting the film to the local newspaper and to the school board. People who saw economic benefit in having the film company in town for two or three weeks and those who hoped to get jobs as extras in the film didn't want the possible benefits to go to another town. The film's producer threatened to sue the school board if they reneged on the agreement. Suddenly, the filming had become a controversial issue.

An overflow crowd attended the school board meeting at which there was to be a debate and a vote on whether approval for the film should be withdrawn. The meeting was raucous. One reporter felt that the behavior of the crowd was rude. She was surprised by the lack of civility at the meeting. There was a lot of booing, jeering, hooting, and rude laughter. Several of the older speakers were interrupted by catcalls and mocking laughter.

"One former teacher," the reporter wrote, "who is probably seventy or older, protested that the script used a four-letter word. She was interrupted by a mocking chorus of young voices."

"No one should have been surprised that the elderly woman was offended by the language in the script," the reporter commented the next day. "I'm saddened by the attitude of these young people toward older citizens."

One reason that the school board voted to withdraw its approval was the behavior of the young people at the meeting.

Do students in your school use bad language? Why?

Are young people openly disrespectful to older people? Why?

What happens in a society when more and more young people are discourteous to the elderly?

Do you think the movie company was able to get a nearby high school to agree to filming on its campus? Why or why not?

CHARACTER

Cupcake

Copyright © Addison-Wesley Educational Publishers, Inc.

Mrs. Francis looked up as Linda came into the living room.
"Hi, honey," Mrs. Francis greeted her daughter.
Linda made a small sound.
"How'd everything go today?"

"I'd rather not talk about it," replied Linda as she headed toward the kitchen.

"Oh," sighed Mrs. Francis. "We'll have dinner at 6:30, Linda."

"I'm not sure if I'll be hungry," Linda said, popping a cupcake into her mouth.

Mrs. Francis glanced into the kitchen. "You won't be if you eat another of those."

"Don't be telling me I eat all the wrong things. I know what's good for me!" Linda retorted.

An hour later, at the dinner table, Mr. Francis tried to engage his daughter in conversation. "Saw an old friend of ours, Linda. Do you remember Jack Sawyer? Of course, you were much younger when you saw him last. Maybe only seven. He hasn't changed much though."

"I'm not interested in him," Linda interrupted.

There was a silence. Mrs. Francis looked at her husband with a half-frown. "What about Jack, dear? Do he and Jane still live on the other side of the river?"

Mr. Francis, abashed, said, "Yes, Myrtle. They're still there."

Then Mrs. Francis turned to Linda and asked, "How are you doing in your math class now, Linda?"

"It's none of your business!" Linda said emphatically. She left the table.

Do you think something was bothering Linda, or do you suppose she always talks that way to her parents?

Do children have a right to talk differently to their parents than to other adults?

What is the relationship of rudeness to respect? Is being rude always a sign of disrespect?

Is there ever a time when being rude is all right?

Nettie Speaks Up

Nettie couldn't stand it any more. Spitwads were flying through the air; students were shouting and laughing; most of the class was out of their seats; and the substitute teacher's face had gone from red to white. What was it now . . . does a star turn from red to blue to white as it heads toward extinction? The extinction of this poor young woman who was substituting for Mrs. Lennox was near at hand, thought Nettie. Either the principal would put a stop to the bedlam or the substitute teacher would run out of the room.

Just one more spitball, thought Nettie, and something will have to happen; the harried teacher wouldn't be able to make it through the last fourteen minutes of the period. Mrs. Lennox had left instructions, but she evidently didn't tell the substitute how to get the kids to cooperate.

"Stop it, you guys!" Nettie found herself shouting. And then, in a lower voice, "Why don't we behave like decent kids? C'mon now, the fun is over. Let's show Ms. Marsden we can behave like civilized people."

Nettie's little speech quieted the class down, but would they erupt again?

Obviously Nettie felt sorry for the substitute teacher, and she probably wasn't the only student to sympathize with Ms. Marsden. Do you think the class settled down for the rest of the period?

If they went back to misbehaving, what do you think Nettie did? What do you think Ms. Marsden did?

What is the difference between sympathy and empathy?

Have you had an experience similar to Nettie's? What did you do?

Did Nettie sympathize or empathize with Ms. Marsden? Could it have been both? Explain.

Follow-Up to "Nettie Speaks Up"

For middle school and junior high school students.
Optional—at the discretion of the teacher.

Although there may be repercussions, you might invite your students to conduct the research activity on page 59. It will make students appreciate teachers and how they have to manage their classes and their time productively. It will also give students practice in calculating percentages.

Getting Ready

If a teacher takes eight minutes of a fifty-five-minute period to bring the class to order, to take attendance, and pass out papers, what percentage of the period is used for noninstructional matters?

During the next school day, glance at the clock at the beginning of all of your classes and note the time it takes before instructional activities begin. Before each class, guess what percentage of time will be devoted to noninstructional matters. Rank your teachers in terms of the amount of time they take to get the class started.

Sounding You Out

Silvio, his younger brother Joe, and three friends had a band. They played electric guitars, drums, trumpet, and saxophone. The band practiced in Silvio and Joe's garage twice a week, on Tuesdays and Thursdays. The garage was close to where the three other band members lived, so it was a convenient place for rehearsing. There was only one problem: the music could be heard for almost a block in every direction. The neighbors didn't complain because they liked the five boys and wanted them to be successful. Nonetheless, a remark or two about the noise reached the ears of Silvio and Joe. Silvio was worried that they were keeping people awake on Tuesdays and Thursdays.

One Thursday the band was practicing for a job coming up the next Saturday. After 11:00, they debated whether to rehearse another hour. Silvio didn't think they should, but Joe and the others wanted to put in extra time. Finally, everyone agreed with Silvio that they could get together the next day for more rehearsing.

Silvio thought more about keeping people awake when they practiced late. He decided that, even though his garage was convenient, it would be better if they used his cousin's barn at the edge of the city for rehearsing. The barn was a hundred yards from the house, so they would disturb only a few sheep. Even though they would have to travel five miles to the barn, the band agreed that traveling was better than disturbing people in the neighborhood.

Once, most people lived in the country, and no one had heard of noise pollution. On a farm, people go to bed early and get up early. Even with tractors and other mechanical equipment, farms are not noisy places. In the city, problems of noise, litter, garbage removal, and unclean air have made the quality of life less wholesome. We are solving some of these problems, but the one problem that stubbornly persists is noise pollution.

What do you think can be done to alleviate the unwelcome sounds of the city?

How can people reduce the amount of unwanted noise in our towns and cities?

CHARACTER MATTERS
Working with Others

In 1971 the people who devised the curriculum for Children Television Workshop's *Sesame Street* decided that it was important to teach cooperation to preschool children. As a result, they devised a series of programs to help children learn how to cooperate with other people.

Developmentally, parallel play precedes cooperation. Some child psychologists firmly believe that the type of social behavior we consider "cooperative" is as much a matter of maturation as of learning. In their view, it is a waste of time to teach the concept before the child is ready.

Before presenting the exercises in this section, you may want to ask the students to discuss the question of whether cooperation and sharing are simply matters of mutual self-interest. Do we cooperate because it is mutually beneficial to do so? Do we share because there is a benefit to both (or all) of the sharers? Do those who give up something benefit?

Trust is basic to any satisfactory relationship, whether business or personal. The problem for all of us, young and old alike, is that we want to be trusted and we know how important it is to feel that someone trusts us, but gaining someone's trust and keeping it is not easy. Once an individual has been let down, if only a little, recapturing that person's trust is extraordinarily difficult. "Trust me" is a familiar line in a funny story because the person saying it obviously can't be completely trusted. But, along with being respected, what is more important than to be trusted?

CHARACTER

Working Together

It takes teamwork to win athletic contests such as those in baseball, basketball, hockey, and football. The team with the stars doesn't always win. On many occasions, a team with the superior personnel has lost to a team that worked well together. That possibility is what makes team sports exciting. Team sports require teamwork—that is, the team members have to operate as a team, not as individuals.

Following are some activities that may or may not benefit from teamwork:

Fighting a flu epidemic

Playing a round of golf

Racing a stock car

Flying an airplane

Removing an appendix

Making a quilt

Doing a crossword puzzle

Preventing the pollution of
rivers and lakes

Running a summer camp

Writing a letter

Shoeing a horse

Mending a barbed-wire fence

Designing a dress

Playing a card game

Walking a dog

Campaigning for public office

In which of these activities is teamwork unnecessary?

In which of these activities is teamwork absolutely necessary?

In which of these activities is teamwork a big advantage?

In which of these activities is teamwork a smaller advantage?

In which of these activities is teamwork impossible?

If you don't know about some of the activities listed, find out about them.

Which of these endeavors is important to society? Why?

Think of an activity that makes your community a good place to live. Are the people you know good team members in this activity? Do their actions help or hurt the community? Why?

Follow-Up to "Working Together"

A follow-up to this unit would be to have your students engage in an activity that requires unified reactions to directions. "Explosive Mirror" emphasizes the importance of listening accurately and responding as a group.

Explosive Mirror

Have the class stand up, and ask for a volunteer to be the leader. The leader should improvise a movement to go with a nonsense sound (e.g., "ooblahdee," "flahdah," "beeyoubah") and then freeze. (It is best to have the class react to the leader in mirror-like fashion, leaning to the left if the leader has leaned to the right.) The group should also freeze, and the leader should spontaneously perform another combination of sound and movement, freezing as the sound ends. The group mirrors the leader's sounds and movements, which can be increasingly challenging but should not be so difficult that most of the students will be unable to follow.

Because the students must pay close attention to the sounds and movements of the leader, this activity is especially valuable for developing skills of responsiveness, concentration, and spontaneity. As in "Simon Says," dancing classes, and military marching, when someone is not moving along with the group, it is readily apparent to everyone, including and especially to the one who is out of step.

The danger in this kind of activity is that a student may be deficient in physical coordination and thus will be continually caught in the wrong position. Be prepared to ease the student's discomfort.

Have a Little Faith (In Me)

Germine wasn't happy with her mother's instruction. She was asked—maybe the word is *ordered*—to have her brother, Regis, teach her how to peel potatoes. Usually Regis got out of these assignments. At eleven, he was three years older than Germine and had managed to escape many of the household chores that used to come his way.

"Well, okay, Regis can help me, but I'm not sure I want to learn anyway," Germine told her mother.

"C'mon, Germine. Let's get this over with," Regis called to his sister.

She sat at the kitchen table opposite him, and he began peeling a potato with a knife.

"You have to dig in here. See that eye? Well, you have to not only cut the skin but dig into the eye like this," Regis instructed Germine.

After two or three more demonstrations, Regis handed the knife to his sister and told her to do what he did. Germine struggled with the knife. She wasn't used to knives, and she was also a little afraid of them. The first potato was a challenge, and at one point Regis groaned loudly. In attacking the second potato, Germine stabbed at an eye but slipped and dug the knife into the table. Regis groaned some more.

While trying to peel the third potato, Germine nearly cut her finger. Regis threw up his hands and said, "I'm not going to watch any more. You're not doing it the way I showed you, and you're going to cut yourself. I'm not going to be responsible!"

Germine put down the knife and made a face at her brother. Then, as he left the kitchen, she began to sob softly.

What was missing in Regis's attitude? How could he have helped Germine have more confidence about peeling potatoes?

When Randy hung up the telephone, he called out to his father, "I got the job, Dad! The Manleys are going to have me look after their pets and yard all next week."

Randy's father smiled and said in a matter-of-fact way, "You'll do a good job, Randy."

"And the money will really help me get that scuba outfit," Randy said.

"Did Mr. Manley show you just what he wants done, Randy?"

"Yeah, he did. And I'm not to give the goldfish too much food. The yard won't be any problem because I know how to water and stuff," replied Randy.

Although he was tempted to, Randy's father didn't check up on his son during the week to see if he was doing everything he was told to do. A year before, Randy had forgotten to water another neighbor's favorite plant, and it had died; but Randy's father knew that his son was conscientious and had learned a lesson. This time Randy had a checklist, and he wouldn't forget a thing.

What do these two stories have in common?

What was missing in the story about Germine and Regis that was present in the story about Randy and his father?

Follow-Up to "Have a Little Faith (In Me)"

Following is a short exercise that you can put on the chalkboard or reproduce on a sheet of paper. It should provoke additional thinking about the idea of trust.

The exercise is an acrostic in reverse. The definitions are supplied, and your students should supply the words that are being defined. Each of the words relates to trust.

The first word to be produced is **truth**, and despite its importance in our language, it is a hard concept to nail down. The second word is **reliability**. Most of your students should have no trouble coming up with **understanding** for the third word. The fourth word is **sincerity**. Perhaps the toughest word to guess is the fifth word, **total**. It is defined as "the amount of confidence needed when you really believe in someone or something." Because it comes last, however, it should be easy to produce the "*t*" after "*t-r-u-s*."

Backward Acrostic

See if you can come up with the five words that are defined below. If you have written words that deal with the same subject, that subject will be spelled out when you look at the first letters of the words you have written.

1.

2.

3.

4.

5.

First word: What we want from the mouths of people we believe in; the opposite of *falsehood*; reality

Second word: A trait that dependable people have

Third word: The basis for being tolerant; a good way of overcoming prejudice

Fourth word: A quality that phony people don't have

Fifth word: The amount of confidence needed when you really believe in someone or something

What word do the first letters spell?

Now close your eyes for a minute. What picture comes into your mind when you think of that word? If the picture isn't clear to you at first, keep your eyes closed a while longer until it is. Why don't you use a pencil and some crayons or colored pencils to draw that picture? First sketch out your ideas, and then make a more detailed drawing. The colors you use will be important to the idea you are trying to convey.

The Tiger

When the Board of Education announced that any student residing in the district could attend any of the district's schools, so long as the student could be transported without causing the district extra expense, some members of the community could see trouble ahead. The four high schools had generally taken turns in establishing winning records in football, volleyball, baseball, softball, and basketball. But there were two new coaches who wanted to dominate the other schools in their sports. One was the volleyball coach at South High. The other was the boys' basketball coach at Reynolds High. They were both young men, and they both wanted to establish outstanding records and then go on to coach at the college level.

Julia's father had gone to Mountain View High, as had his father. In fact, most of Julia's relatives had attended Mountain View. No one was surprised when she became the star of the Mountain View freshman volleyball team because she was tall and her father had been an all-state basketball player for Mountain View.

Julia and her family decided it might be a good idea for her to attend a volleyball camp in the summer. Tom Sperling, the head volleyball coach from South High, was running the camp. Tom gave Julia special attention, especially when he saw that she was the best player in the camp.

By the end of the last week of camp, Tom Sperling had approached Julia twice about transferring to South High. He presented her with a rosy picture of joining a team that was on the brink of greatness (they'd come in second in the league), and of then getting a scholarship to a four-year college. Tom was a good salesman, and Julia was almost convinced by the time she returned home.

When Julia told her father about Tom Sperling's pitch for Julia to transfer to South, he asked her what her year at Mountain View had been like and how well she liked her classmates and teachers. Julia replied that she liked everything at Mountain View. Then he asked her if she thought that being at South High would really increase her chances of getting a scholarship. Mountain View's varsity team, the Tigers, had been third in the league, and Julia could help them move up in the standings next year. Julia told her father she would think about her dilemma and then make a decision.

At the breakfast table the next morning, Julia gave her father the thumbs-up sign. "I was born to be a Tiger, Dad, and I'm always going to be one," she said in a happy voice.

Do you think that Julia received a scholarship offer when she graduated?

Was she being more loyal to her school or to her family when she decided to stay at Mountain View? Explain.

John Yee, a classmate of Julia's, had arrived with his family from Southeast Asia only three years before, but his ambition was to attend MIT or Cal Tech. Since Reynolds High's math department was regarded as superior to the math departments of the other three high schools, John was considering transferring to Reynolds from Mountain View.

Would John's transfer mean that he wasn't being loyal to Mountain View?

Nelda Pitts, another sophomore at Mountain View, was a fair student, but she was a talented singer and actress. Mountain View's drama department put on two plays a year, and the drama teacher was also the journalism teacher and adviser. Nelda felt that she didn't have sufficient opportunities to display her talents at Mountain View. Her family history, however, went back farther than did Julia's when it came to being a Tiger. Her great-grandfather had been in the first graduating class.

Would Nelda be disloyal if she were to transfer to Meredith High, where the drama teacher was the driving force behind most of the city's summer musicals and plays?

CHARACTER

Agony

Fourteen-year-old Michael stood still as his mother screamed at him. A man and a woman were pushing her into a car. It was a sheriff's car, and the man and woman were deputies. Michael had phoned the sheriff's department, asking for help.

For the past week, Michael's mother had been taking drugs and drinking liquor. She was acting crazy, and he couldn't do anything with her. He could stand her not cooking meals and making a mess of the house, but he couldn't stand to see what she was doing to herself.

Nothing in his young life had been so painful for Michael. But he knew he was doing the right thing. His mother needed help badly, and he couldn't provide the help she needed. As the car pulled away, Michael's mother looked back at her son and muttered something he couldn't hear. Her face made her sentiments clear, though.

Was Michael being disloyal to his mother? Explain.

What does being loyal to a troubled relative or friend entail?

The Blue Sweater

Tiffany had some misgivings but she finally let her best friend, Kate, borrow her new blue sweater to wear to the church picnic. Tiffany had been reluctant to loan the sweater because it had been given to her by her favorite uncle and she knew Kate didn't take good care of her own clothes.

On Monday, Tiffany didn't see Kate at their usual meeting place in the cafeteria. They didn't have any classes together in the morning, so they usually got together at lunch. Tiffany didn't give too much thought to Kate's absence, but she wanted to know how the church picnic turned out. They did have a social studies class together after noon recess, though, and Tiffany found Kate in her regular seat. Kate wasn't enthusiastic about the picnic when Tiffany asked about it. In fact, Kate didn't want to talk about the picnic at all.

Tiffany didn't concern herself with Kate's behavior until, at the end of the school day, she asked Kate when she'd be returning the blue sweater. At first Kate was evasive, but then a sob crept into her voice, and she confessed that a spark from a fire had flown on to the sweater, and now it had a big hole in the front. Tiffany was horrified. It was her favorite sweater, and it was ruined.

She just turned away from Kate and began walking toward the school bus. Kate stood still, and her eyes began to fill with tears.

The girls didn't meet in the cafeteria for the rest of the week. On Monday Tiffany came early to social studies and waited at Kate's desk. When Kate came in, she avoided Tiffany's eyes.

"It's okay, Kate," Tiffany began. "I know you didn't want to hurt my sweater. It wasn't your fault that a spark got on it. I understand."

Kate threw her arms around Tiffany's neck.

Tiffany had reasoned that her friendship with Kate was more important to her than the blue sweater. She could get another sweater, but she wasn't sure she could find another friend as good as Kate.

What is the opposite of being forgiving?

If a person never forgives another for doing something, what happens then?

What is a vendetta?

In some countries, vendettas last for many generations. What do we have in this country that is the same as a vendetta?

What can be done about disputes that go on and on?

No

*J*on guessed that Geraldine was going to ask him to her party. Geraldine hesitated to ask Jon because she was afraid he'd give an excuse about why he couldn't come. Geraldine guessed that Jon's friend, Pete, would know what Jon would say. Peter guessed that Jon would say that he'd go to the party. Peter guessed wrong.

Maybe there was too much guessing going on. On the other hand, Geraldine had a good reason to be uncertain about Jon's reception of her invitation. It's no fun to be rejected, and Geraldine wanted to avoid that embarrassment.

In each of the situations below there is a possibility of a rejection. Tell how you would react to these situations, and then explain your reasons for reacting in those ways.

Your teacher invites you to be master of ceremonies at the talent show next month. If you refuse, are you rejecting the teacher or the offer to be master of ceremonies?

A student you know only slightly asks you to dance at a school dance. What do you do if the student isn't very attractive?

Is the person asking you to dance risking anything? Put yourself in the place of that person. Could it be deflating to be turned down?

Although you are stuck on a math problem, you don't like to admit that you don't know how to do it. Your teacher sees that you are having trouble and asks you if the brightest math student in class might help you. How do you feel about the offer of help?

How would the teacher feel if you declined the offer?

How would the bright student feel if he or she has overheard the teacher's offer?

What might be the consequences if these items are rejected?

A shot at the buzzer
Candy
Praise
A ring
A cigarette
A lie
A sweater
Revenge
Flowers
Truth

Explain how a rejection could result in each of these outcomes:

A good night's sleep
A safer trip
A ticket to the circus
Mold in the refrigerator
Increased respect
A bankruptcy
Spilled milk
A victory
A broken pencil
A treaty
A soiled hat
A drowning
Dizziness
A successful career

On a separate piece of paper write a short story about one of the situations above. You already have the basis for a plot in your explanations. You can use the space below to outline your plot.

CHARACTER

Together

When Gene was a boy, it bothered him that his family didn't do things together. Gene saw other families going on hikes and rides, going on picnics, and going to the movies. He and his sister occasionally walked to school together, but since she was two years older than Gene, she didn't confide in him about her hopes or her enthusiasms. So Gene didn't share his innermost feelings, or even his complaints, with his sister.

"It's going to be different when I get married," Gene vowed. And it was. When Gene married Barbara, he wanted to do everything with her. The only time they were apart was when he was working at his job. If Barbara had to get a loaf of bread at the store five blocks away, he'd come with her. If Gene wanted to go bowling, they got into a mixed league so that they could be on the same team. If Gene volunteered to help at the Boy Scouts pancake breakfast, Barbara was there to take tickets at the door while he flipped pancakes. They were inseparable.

Some married couples insist on having separate interests so that they won't get on each other's nerves by being together too much. It depends on the individuals. In many ways, Gene and Barbara led an ideal existence because they could share so much of both the good and bad things in life.

Here are some of the experiences, emotions, things, and people we can share:

Loved ones	Ice cream	Games
Grief	Clothing	A hero
Friends	A prejudice	Fear
Watching television	Songs	An enthusiasm
Gossip	Popcorn	Pets

Is it more important to you to have someone share the good things or to share the bad things? Explain.

Give an example of each and explain why you would or would not like to share it with others.

Loved ones

Grief

Friends

Watching television

Gossip

Ice cream

Clothing

A prejudice

Songs

Popcorn

Games

A hero

Fear

An enthusiasm

Pets

CHARACTER MATTERS
Attitudes

So much is said and written about prejudice and stereotyping that the units in this section may seem old hat to a youngster of eleven or twelve. Accordingly, with the exception of "Knock It Off!", you probably won't have to lead in to these units with much of an introduction or warm-up.

The story in "Knock It Off!" is about a young boy who unthinkingly kills honeybees and is scolded by two older boys. Children routinely kill bugs and other small creatures. It seems that children have to learn a different attitude when it comes to respecting small forms of life. There is a good chance that the idea of not killing a bee or a spider will surprise some of your students. No one defends the right of a fly or a mosquito to live, and it may seem odd to a youngster to learn that spiders and bees are beneficial to us. It's almost the reverse of Oscar Hammerstein's moving lyric from *South Pacific*,

"You've Got to Be Carefully Taught," which tells us that people learn to be prejudiced. In this case, a child has to be taught to change his or her attitude about killing every very small creature encountered. Incidentally, because of disease, honeybees are in trouble throughout North America. We need every one of them.

The message of "Smaller May Be Better" is that paying less attention to the ways in which we differ from others can help us live more harmoniously in our communities. There is a strong sentiment among a growing number of groups to celebrate their differences. A number of these groups, not all of which are ethnic or religious, will come readily to your mind. A provocative question for you to ask your students is: With this emphasis on diversity and pride in being different, are we becoming a more tolerant or more intolerant people?

CHARACTER

Insected Minds

You may have heard the expression, "He has a mind like a steel trap." It is supposed to be a compliment about someone's ability to retain information. But, as analogues for the mind, insects may be more satisfactory than machines. For example, a "grasshopper mind" indicates liveliness and uncertainty.

How do you feel about comparing human minds to insects? Usually, to call someone an insect is to insult her or him. But insects have a lot going for them. See if you can complete these sentences:

_____ has the disposition of a rattlesnake and the mind of a flea.

Her mind, as busy as a bee, _____

His grasshopper mind _____

His mind reminds me of a termite because _____

Like a butterfly, his mind _____

Even allowing for her mosquito-like mind, _____

As single-minded as a moth, she _____

Is there an insect you could compare with your own mind? If so, what is it?

Which insects might suggest the minds of these people?

Lawyers

Accountants

Security guards

Forest rangers

Salespeople

Inventors

Beauticians

Why have you characterized these people as you have? Is it because you have heard people speak of them in certain ways? Do we tend to stereotype such workers as used-car salesmen and lawyers? Take your list and ask three adults and three young people if they agree with the insects you have compared to the seven workers. Write the results of your survey below.

Not All of It

GRRRR

Some statements that people make are partially true. There is an element of truth in them, but they aren't totally true. Examine the following statements carefully, and then talk over each one with a classmate. Decide whether the statements are true, false, or partly true.

Since Billy Mills and José Pihra were Native Americans and were great long-distance runners, all Native Americans are good at running long distances.

Having won several competitions, Terrence Baily is an excellent marksman with a pistol, so he must have a steady hand and good vision.

A person who passes a driver's license test and is given a license is not necessarily a safe driver.

Since none of the world's first-ranked orchestras is conducted by a woman, men are better conductors of orchestras than are women.

The ancient Mayan Indians performed rituals in which young women were put to death as sacrifices to gods, and so we know that the Mayans valued girls less than boys.

Most of the great advances in the physical sciences have come about in the past 200 years, and the majority of them have been the work of Americans.

If dogs don't like certain people, those people can't be trusted.

Tall men make better leaders because they are more impressive-looking.

Most lawyers are good at taking advantage of situations in which they can use their knowledge to make a lot of money.

Overweight people are naturally easy-going and jolly.

Crazy As a Loon

If you really want to know, the cuckoo isn't cuckoo and the loon isn't loony. The cuckoo is clever, not crazy, in depositing her eggs in the nests of other birds. The loon is as sane as the cuckoo; it just has a weird call. On the other hand, the fox is sly, or foxy, and the ox is dumb, or relatively unintelligent. Some animals deserve their reputations, and some don't.

Do these workers really deserve their reputations? Explain why or why not.

Are used-car salespeople untrustworthy? Do you know one that isn't? Who is he or she?

Why are used-car salespeople considered dishonest?

Are all artists eccentric? Do you know one that isn't?
Who is she or he?

Why are artists considered peculiar or different?

Are barbers and beauticians really gabby? Do you know one that isn't?
Who is he or she?

Why are they considered very talkative?

Are dentists usually unsympathetic? Do you know one that is quite
sympathetic? Who is she or he?

Why do people think dentists are indifferent to other people's pain?

What would happen if dentists showed too much sympathy?

Are lawyers always mercenary? Do you know one that isn't money hungry?
Who is he or she?

Do lawyers deserve their reputation as mercenary professionals?

Explain why.

Are most professors absent-minded? Do you know one that isn't? Who is she or he?

Why do you think professors have the reputation of being absent-minded?

Are actors always vain?   Do you know an actor who isn't vain?
Who is he or she? How do you know that the actor isn't vain or conceited?

What is it called when we lump a group of people into one category, such as
labeling all used-car salespeople as untrustworthy or dishonest?

What other groups are ordinarily stereotyped in your community?

Copyright © Addison-Wesley Educational Publishers, Inc.

CHARACTER

Smaller May Be Better

 e may or may not like it, but the world is getting smaller. Television sets, pedigreed dogs, magazines, and many other things are being produced in smaller versions.

What would you like to make smaller?

Your troubles?

A friend's ego?

Your appetite?

How could we make these smaller?

Bills

Waistlines

Lectures by parents

Forest fires

Number of traffic accidents

Homework

Number of bankruptcies

Number of cavities

Size of the national debt

Epidemics

Being tolerant is really minimizing—making smaller—your differences with others. The differences are less important to you when you are tolerant. If someone puts green dye on her hair, you can reflect that there is a wide variation in hair styles now and that those matters are not as important as kindness, trust, and honesty.

How can we make these differences in others smaller, or less important, to us?

Body sizes

Body shapes

Dress

Athletic abilities

Religious beliefs

Food preferences

Musical preferences

Wealth

Is it true that if a person is intolerant, he or she wants to make more of his or her differences with others?

Knock It Off!

On a lovely day in September, Frank and Norris were heading for a playground, hoping to find others interested in a pickup game of basketball. As the boys turned a corner about a block from the playground, they saw a younger boy, about nine, doing something at a flowering bush near a walk leading to a house. At first Norris and Frank didn't pay much attention to the boy, who was of medium height for his age and rather stocky. Then Frank remarked, "I think that kid's hitting something with a little paddle."

Norris said, "It looks like he's swatting bees."

"Yeah, that's what he's doing—he's killing bees!" Frank said. "He shouldn't be doing that!"

Norris walked over to the boy and said quietly, "Why are you hitting those bees? Do you realize that you're killing them?"

"Yeah. It's fun. I try to see how far they'll go when I hit them," the boy answered.

"Bees do a lot of good, and they won't bother you if you don't bother them!" Frank exclaimed.

"Knock it off, kid!" Norris ordered. "Find something else to hit besides bees. We need them."

The boy looked up at Norris and Frank and then walked up to the house.

What are the two main reasons that we need bees?

Do you think that the boy went back to swatting bees when Norris and Frank left? Explain why or why not.

The amount of harm the little boy can do is negligible compared to the countless bees in the world. Why should anyone worry about what he does to twenty or thirty bees?

CHARACTER MATTERS
Concern for the Community

This section comes close to defining the outward manifestations of what a good citizen is by dealing with such matters as charity, public service, and civic responsibility. Perhaps more than the other sections, it affords natural springboards for further discussion and investigation. For example, questions about the misuse of funds are posed in "From Scooters to Squash." The revelations that some charitable organizations give a large proportion of their funds to businesses that solicit money for them and that they pay high-powered executives huge salaries have proved surprising—even shocking—to many citizens.

Not many towns can be operated solely by volunteers ("For the Good of the Town"), but there is a lot more volunteerism in our communities than you might think. Connections for Independent Living is a relatively unknown program of the American Association of Retired

Persons (AARP) that utilizes the talents of senior citizens. It links AARP volunteers to community agencies that help older people remain in their homes, and it encourages community service projects.

Of the six units in this section, "Intervention" offers the most opportunity for both philosophical debate and practical research. Many of the situations listed should be familiar to your students, and they may have actually had chances to intervene in similar situations. This unit should be presented after your students have had opportunities to think about what constitutes ethical behavior and what is involved in having a social conscience.

From Scooters to Squash

When Nathan's family moved into their new home, he was delighted by the big backyard. There was so much bare ground, in fact, that he immediately made a track for his motor scooter. He put two ramps on it and curved the track so it would be fun to see how fast he could make the circuit. The track drew the attention of several kids in the neighborhood, and soon Nathan had acquired a few friends and a lot of acquaintances.

The next year, Nathan had lost interest in his motor scooter and put in a vegetable garden. He'd always been fascinated with growing plants, and, besides, he loved corn, carrots, beans, squash, and peas. Nathan's vegetable garden was a huge success. In fact, it was too good, and he had to spend time giving away his surplus vegetables.

The following spring, remembering the bounty from last year, Nathan's mother asked him if he were going to grow more vegetables. She would do some canning, she said, but canning wasn't her favorite pastime.

"I don't know, Mom," Nathan said. "I kinda got the feeling I was forcing vegetables on the neighbors. You know, I've been reading about all of the homeless people and the churches not having enough food in their food bank to feed them. There's always a food drive going on in town. Do you suppose my vegetables would help?"

"Yes, I do, Nathan. That sounds like a good idea. You can be giving the food bank vegetables all through the summer and fall. These people around here appreciated you giving them fresh vegetables, but they certainly didn't need them. The homeless do."

Seven of the churches in Nathan's town had been housing and feeding the homeless for several years. What organizations are doing that kind of charitable work in your community?

Some charitable organizations have been charged with using too much of their funds for administrative expenses and fund-raising. Look into this matter and find out which national organizations have been guilty of using a substantial proportion of their funds for administrators' salaries, promotional activities, and plush accommodations. List them below.

Follow-Up to "From Scooters to Squash"

The following exercise, "Improve Your World," will heighten your students' sensitivity to the plight of people who are in unfortunate circumstances. Throughout the country there are increasing numbers of individuals, young and old, who hold up signs asking for food or jobs. In some cities senior citizens have organized to glean food from fields and orchards. That activity is a relatively recent development, and it tells us that we have food resources and human resources that can help alleviate hunger in our society. Young people can help too.

Improve Your World

Sometimes we see streets and buildings that need repairing, but we think to ourselves that it is someone else's responsibility to fix them. On the other hand, when roads and buildings are hazardous to people, we can call the authorities to let them know.

These days we often see people who are homeless and people with signs offering to work for food. In small ways we can help by giving money and food to people in need. In many cities there are food banks and kitchens that serve people who are in unfortunate circumstances. You can contribute to food drives or help deliver the food. You might also have an idea about conserving and preserving food that isn't being saved now.

If you have thought of a way to conserve or preserve food, what is it?

What food would you make more appealing or more abundant by changing a recipe for its preparation? After thinking about a food that can be made better or more appealing or that can be stretched to feed more people, do some research about it and then experiment in a kitchen. After you have tested it, write your recipe below

For the Good of the Town

Dog

Dog Catcher

Not too long ago, the little town of San Juan Bautista in California went broke. The town owed more money than it had in its treasury. The paid officials had to resign, but most of them stayed on their jobs without pay. The citizens of this town decided that they could perform all of the services that were needed by enlisting volunteers. People young and old maintained equipment, cleaned the streets, collected garbage, maintained the parks and playgrounds, fought the fires, and kept the peace.

What other jobs did they have to do?

All of the merchants volunteered their services when the plan was proposed. Why do you think they did so?

Which of the many jobs done by the volunteers probably was most difficult to carry out?

The good part about volunteerism is that it gives a person a chance to give something back to his or her community. The bad part about volunteerism is that the volunteer is not getting paid and so feels free to quit—sometimes at a moment's notice. It is hard to run a volunteer organization: what if a volunteer does unsatisfactory work or fails to show up?

Imagine that you are one of the volunteers in charge of collecting garbage in San Juan Bautista. One of your volunteer workers has not shown up to collect garbage for two out of the last three Wednesdays, when people put their garbage on the curbs for pickup. Each time this volunteer fails to do the job, people complain, and you have to do the work yourself. What are you going to do?

You can examine this problem by doing some role-playing with two other students. One student can be the supervisor, another can be the mayor, and the third student can take the part of the irresponsible volunteer.

Follow-Up to "For the Good of the Town"

We often look at animals and see human characteristics in their actions and even in their looks. You can capitalize on this human trait to get your students to think about the people who serve their communities (often in spite of criticism and hardship).

Play "Carnival of the Animals" by Saint-Saens on a tape recorder or phonograph, and have your students identify the animals without any prompting or cues. After the animals have been identified, your students can portray them in pantomime. Then ask them to think of what roles those animals might play in a city of animals. Would one of them be a good police officer? Which one might be the mayor? Which could be the fire chief? Would one of the animals would make a good actor?

Many familiar animals are not portrayed by Saint-Saens, of course, and you might invite your students to depict other animals with rhythm instruments, the piano, or other instruments of their choice. Ask them what kind of music would be particularly appropriate for an animal representing some person who particularly contributes to the good of the community—a minister or rabbi, a street cleaner, the director of parks and recreation, or a librarian.

Expectations

Life is structured by expectations. They allow us to go ahead with our routines, with our plans; but they also are responsible for blowups, misunderstandings, snafus, tragedies, and disasters.

What expectations do you have about tomorrow, besides the universal ones that the sun will rise and that you will have to wake up?

When we have definite expectations of others, it frees us to act in certain ways. On the other hand, when the expectations derive from incorrect information or preconceptions, trouble can ensue. For example, when someone who has always been punctual in the past is late, you may become upset. Yet you yourself may often be late for school, appointments, and social affairs. Likewise, you might go to a party dressed formally and discover that everyone else is dressed casually. Because of your attendance at similar parties, your expectation was that this party would be a formal affair. Such an experience is unsettling.

Groups of people also have to rely on sets of expectations in dealing with other groups. Trouble often arises when one group doesn't know what another group might do.

What could be the situation that caused an expectation to turn into a

reconciliation?

prize?

humorous incident?

tragedy?

mishap?

fight?

war?

comedy?

labor dispute?

friendship?

Think of a dispute that has occurred recently in your community. You should be able to find an account of one in your local newspaper. Then see if part or all of the dispute stemmed from a misunderstanding because of erroneous expectations. What was the dispute?

Were there any false or misleading expectations on either side (or on both sides)? What were they?

Follow-Up to "Expectations"

In order to make the unit more personal to your students, you might inquire about their experiences in improving their community. Ask which students are regularly involved in activities that contribute to the good of the community. In most classrooms there are students who are members of the Scouts, YMCA or YWCA, CYO, Jewish youth organizations, and other groups. You can also ask if any of your students have parents or siblings who contribute in some way to the welfare of the people in the community.

It might be most effective to have students interview other students about their or their family members' service to the community. A tape recorder can be used in conducting the interviews. The tape-recorded interviews can be reviewed by the class after they have been conducted in private.

Even if many of your students are familiar with the organizations that serve the community, it would be a wonderful idea to have the class visit nursing homes, homeless shelters, soup kitchens, hospitals, and pet shelters. In many communities, young people volunteer on a regular basis in such organizations, and you'll have a guide from your class if a student is actively engaged. It is also a good idea to visit organizations that don't elicit much enthusiasm from your students during the discussion. The ones they might avoid are possibly the ones they should see.

Poisonally

What poisons are you frequently exposed to? Can you name three or four?

What items in the home are locked up or put out of the reach of toddlers?

If a toddler accidentally ingests something that is poisonous, what should be done? If you don't know the answer, find out.

What foods that people commonly eat can be poisonous to certain individuals?

The right action or the correct antidote can save a life. What is the correct antidote for an overdose of nicotine?

Of alcohol?

Of aspirin?

What might be a special antidote for these social poisons?

Hatred

Ignorance

Suspicion

Hostility

Fear

Arrogance

Bigotry

Get together with three or four of your classmates and put together a skit that portrays the antidote for one of those social poisons.

CHARACTER

Three Scenes

H ere are three scenes of individuals interacting. Let's suppose that in each situation you are just out of earshot. Although you can see what is going on, you can't hear the conversation.

Scene 1

Three little girls approach the swings at a playground. There are just two swings, and two of the girls run to the swings. The third girl stands aside and watches. The girls on the swings chatter for about fifteen minutes, and the third girl just watches. Suddenly, they jump off the swings and race over to the slide. The other girl sits down and starts to pull dandelions from the grass, tearing each flower into bits.

Why did the three girls behave this way?

Scene 2

By the time the little red-headed boy had arrived at the teacher's desk, almost every desk behind him had been disrupted. He had pulled papers and books off the desks, grabbed a pencil and then thrown it back at a girl, mussed up the hair of a small boy, and pinched the arm of a girl. The classroom continued to function despite his actions. Even the teacher had hardly looked up as the red-headed boy proceeded down the aisle, making mischief.

Why were there only a few words of protest from the boy's victims? Why didn't the teacher try to stop him as he went down the aisle annoying his classmates?

Scene 3

A stocky boy with short blond hair pedaled down a narrow street lined by yards littered with toys, rubbish, cars, and car parts. After he had proceeded halfway down the block, a slightly smaller boy about his age turned toward the cyclist and then took a couple of steps off the sidewalk into the street.

The boy on foot yelled at the blond boy as he approached on his bike. The cyclist didn't speed up or slow down but looked straight ahead as he passed the smaller boy. Once again, the boy yelled at the blond youngster on the bike, who didn't turn his head or say anything.

Why was the boy on foot yelling at the blond boy on the bicycle?

Was the cyclist in his own neighborhood? Why do you think so?

What might have happened if he hadn't been on his bicycle?

CHARACTER

Intervention

There are times when good citizens do not turn their backs on a scene that calls for action. When people discover that a fire has started in a building, nearly everyone will call 9-1-1 or notify someone. There are other times when it is a little harder to know what one's civic responsibilities are, as in the case of coming upon two men fighting at a street corner. In some situations, it is best to allow the combatants to resolve their differences, as happens when two brothers who are otherwise devoted to each other are tussling. If you don't know the young men are brothers, you can get into trouble.

Here is a list of situations in which a citizen can either ignore what is going on or take some action:

A bridge has just been washed out as a result of a storm.

A tornado is sighted heading toward town.

A young person is observed shoplifting.

An older person is observed shoplifting.

A swimmer is washed out to sea by an undertow or riptide.

A person is seen breaking into a house.

Vandals are seen wrecking the restrooms in a park.

A city official is overheard taking a bribe from a contractor in a restaurant.

A man in a car is observed giving a packet of drugs to two young girls a half-block from a school.

A homeless person is seen rummaging through a dumpster behind a grocery store.

Three large young men are seen taking newspapers out of a newspaper rack; when one pays, the other two grab "free" newspapers.

Two boys are discovered spraying graffiti on a billboard at 3:00 A.M.

An avalanche has just started at the top of a mountain.

Which situations call for only a warning of some kind?

Which situations call for immediate action as well as putting out an alarm?

Which situations call for immediate action only?

With two or more classmates, select one of these situations and dramatize it. In that way, you and your classmates can determine how easy or hard it is to intervene and what the implications are.

CHARACTER MATTERS
Putting It Together

Although the order in which the units are presented in this book is not meant to suggest any particular sequencing, "Hypothetically Speaking," "In the Future," and "Tennis, Anyone?" are placed at the end deliberately. These three units cover most, if not all, of the concepts presented in *Character Matters*. Two of the three come at the concepts in an oblique way, but "In the Future" is quite direct in its approach.

"Hypothetically Speaking" consists of three brief stories about an encyclopedia salesman, a singer, and a takeout clerk and checker at a supermarket. The behavior of each is puzzling. Students are invited to offer explanations for the events in the three stories. One hypothesis is that all three people had trouble showing respect.

"In the Future" consists of ten predictions about the twenty-first century. The statements touch on prestige, discrimination, respect, prejudice, and civic-mindedness. If it can be done naturally, encourage your students to debate any of the statements that "push their buttons." Again, respect is a strong element in this unit.

The last unit may seem far out. Comparing tennis or golf to life is to take to an extreme the current fad of using the language of sports to describe nonathletic activities. The metaphor could hardly be grander or more ambitious. Therefore, we recommend that "Tennis, Anyone?" culminate the units of *Character Matters*. If you believe it is beyond the capabilities of most of your students, use it as an optional exercise. One thing is certain—students who give it a wholehearted effort will be using their brains and imaginations.

Hypothetically Speaking

Here are three cases that, on the surface, are quite perplexing.

Case 1

A young encyclopedia salesman is promoted to supervisor of the salespeople in his region. All but one of the salespeople in the region are women. He lasts only one month, and then he is back selling encyclopedias in his old territory. During that month, business was very good.

What happened? What is your best guess about why the young man only lasted as supervisor for one month?

Case 2

Matilda Jones is a wonderful singer. A soprano with a wide vocal range, she is in demand as a soloist with symphony orchestras, and she also gives many recitals. Last spring, she married her manager, Art Best, who is fifteen years older than Matilda. Art had been married twice before. In the fall, Matilda was unable to keep some of her commitments to sing with orchestras, and she cancelled all of her recitals for the remainder of the year. Not only were a great many people disappointed by these actions but Matilda's income was reduced severely.

What could have been the reason for Matilda's not fulfilling her commitments?

Case 3

Marcus is a dependable employee of the giant supermarket in his town. He has been a takeout clerk and part-time checker for over a year now. Known for his courteous and affable manner, Marcus is liked by his fellow employees and especially by the customers. One day last week, Marcus was substituting for a checker who was ill. Marcus had substituted for her before, and no one was concerned about his doing a good job. Suddenly, at five o'clock in the afternoon, Marcus began shouting at an elderly lady whose groceries he was putting in bags. His voice grew louder. Then, in seeming confusion, the woman left her groceries and ran out the door into the parking lot.

What do you suppose happened? Why would Marcus shout at the woman, and why would she leave the supermarket without her groceries?

CHARACTER

In The Future

There will be changes in society in the future, but will those changes allow us to live more harmoniously? Place a "T" (for true) or an "F" (for false) to the left of these statements, and then tell why you have answered them as you have.

_____ More respect will be given to doctors in the twenty-first century.
There will be less discrimination when hiring minorities.

_____ Fewer people will drive luxury cars in order to impress their friends and neighbors.

_____ A greater percentage of the "worse" jobs, that is, those that have the least prestige, will be taken by immigrants.

_____ People who don't play golf will be looked down upon.

_____ The police will be more respected.

_____ The number of lawyer jokes will continue to increase as there are more and more lawyers.

_____ Fewer and fewer civic-minded people will run for public office because politicians are held in low esteem.

_____ Because of the objections of women's groups, there will be no statewide or national beauty contests.

_____ Artists will be treated with more respect.

Tennis, Anyone?

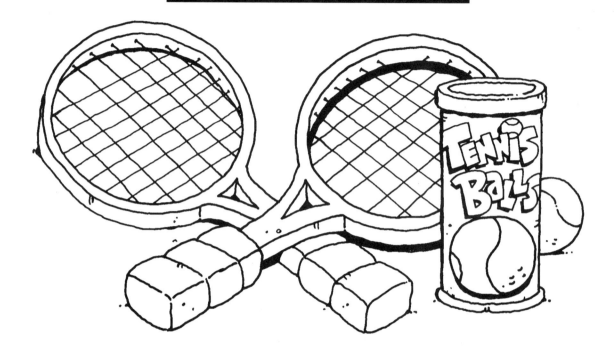

A man was overheard to say, "That's life. It's just like tennis. In fact, there is very little difference between the two games." The man was saying that life is a game, and, moreover, he was comparing it to a game of tennis. Since our language is full of analogies and metaphors about games (e.g., "players," "raising the bar," "the ball's in your court," "level playing field," and so on), his assertion isn't so surprising. Life has been compared to a game by a great many people throughout the ages.

If life is a game, what are the rules of life?

If life is a game, is there a winner? Explain.

If life is a game, is there a loser? Explain.

If life is a game of tennis, what is analogous to the ball? Explain.

What game is like taking a hike? Why is it like taking a hike?

What game is like dancing? Why is it like dancing?

What game is like driving a car? Why is it like driving a car?

What game is like baking bread? Why is it like baking bread?

What activity in life is like baseball? Explain why they are alike.

What activity in life is like running a marathon? Explain why they are alike.

What activity in life is like a wrestling match? Explain why they are alike.

What activity in life is like basketball? Why are they alike?

What activity in life is like a relay race? Explain why they are alike.

What activity in life is like soccer? Why are they alike?

What activity in life is like playing a game of solitaire? Why do you think so?

Another man, considered by his friends to be a cynic, contends that life is more like golf than tennis. Why does he think so, and why does his contention brand him as a cynic?